How Matter works

by Christian Downey

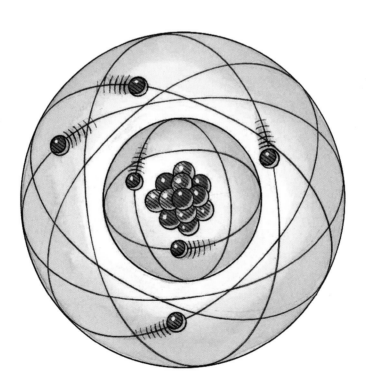

PEARSON
Scott
Foresman

DK

What Matter Is

Look around your classroom. Everything you see is matter. The tables, chairs, books, and people are matter. So are the tiniest pieces of dirt and dust. **Matter** is anything that takes up space and has mass.

Everything around you is matter. That includes the air you breathe. You usually can't see the air you breathe. But don't be fooled. Air is matter!

All objects are made of matter. But not all objects are the same. Look around your classroom again. Some objects are big. Others are small. Some objects are heavy. Others are light. Some objects are hard and some are soft.

Each object has its own special properties. A **property** is a quality of matter that can be observed. You can observe properties with your senses.

By observing matter's properties, you can learn about how things are different. Touching, smelling, and looking at objects helps you learn about their properties.

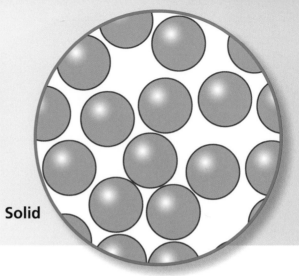

The particles are different in each form of matter.

Solid

Liqui

Forms of Matter

Matter comes in three forms. These forms are solid, liquid, and gas. All three forms are made up of particles, or very small parts. The particles are too small for you to see. But they are always moving. How much they move depends on the form of matter.

Solids

Are you sitting at a desk as you read this? If so, touch the desk. It's pretty hard, right? The desk is a solid. A solid has a shape that doesn't change. Objects such as walls, lamps, and rocks are all solids. The particles in solids keep their shape because their particles are firmly held together.

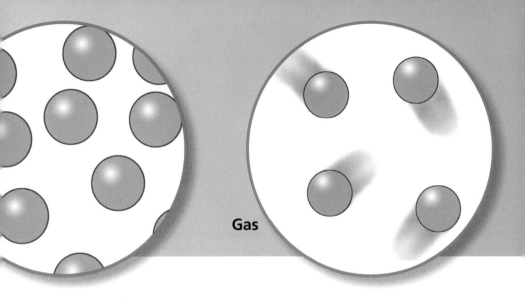

Gas

Liquids

Milk poured into a glass has a shape. The milk had a different shape when it was in the carton. Why did its shape change?

Milk is a liquid. Liquids change shape to match the space they fill. If you pour the milk into a bowl, it will change shape again. No matter what a liquid is poured into, it will always take up the same amount of space. Only the shape will change.

Compared to solids, the particles in liquids are farther apart. But they are still held together. The particles in liquids move around easily.

Gases

Matter can also be a gas. Gases are shapeless. The particles in gas are not connected. They bounce around.

Air is an example of a gas. Blow air into a paper bag. What happens? The bag fills up with the air. The air's **pressure** pushes out the bag's sides.

Gases will take up as much space as they can. If you let the air out, the bag changes its shape!

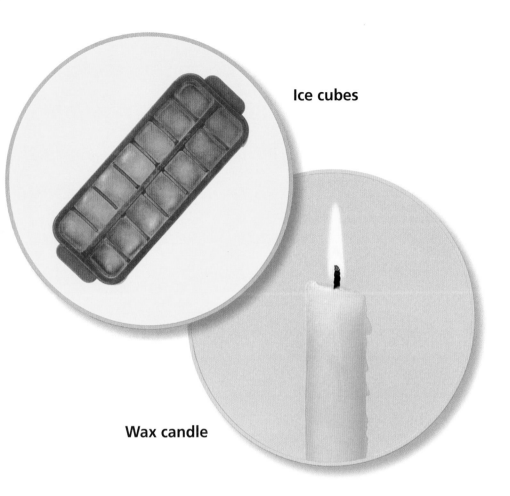

Ice cubes

Wax candle

Some matter can change forms. Water is liquid. It freezes when the temperature drops below thirty-two degrees Fahrenheit. Water freezes to become a solid ice cube.

Candles, like water, also can change form. Candles start as a solid. Their wax melts when it is heated. When that happens, candles turn into liquid. Both water and candles change forms if their temperatures change enough.

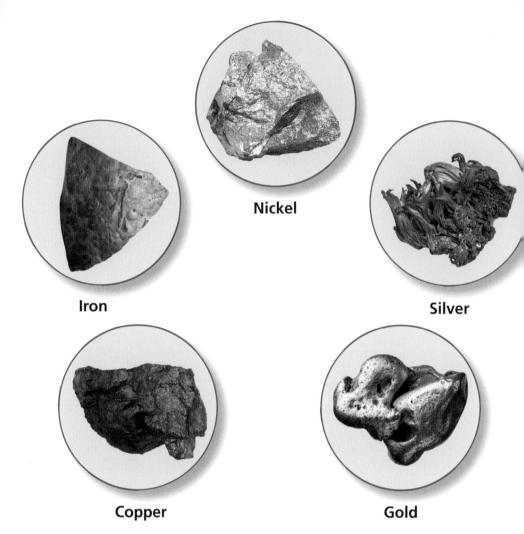

Nickel

Iron

Silver

Copper

Gold

Elements

A piece of silver can be broken into smaller and smaller pieces. No matter how small you make them, they will still be silver. Silver is an element. An **element** is matter that is made of a single kind of particle. Each element's particles are too small to see. Iron, gold, copper, and nickel are all elements.

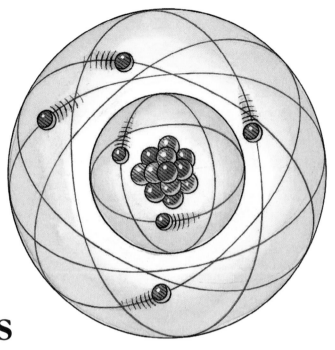

Atoms

Elements can be broken into atoms. An **atom** is a tiny particle of an element. It still has all the properties of that element. One atom of carbon has all the properties of carbon.

There are more than one hundred elements. Each element has its own properties. Elements that have similar properties are sometimes called "families." The **periodic table** is a table that lists elements based on their properties. Elements listed in the same column have similar properties. Each element gets its own box on the periodic table. This box shows the element's symbol and name.

Mass

Mass is the amount of matter an object has. All solids, liquids, and gases have mass. Mass is measured in grams. Grams are the metric unit for mass.

A balance is used to measure and compare the mass of matter. Put some rocks on one side of a balance. Place some feathers on the other side. What happens? The rocks have more mass. Their side of the balance will lower. The feathers have less mass. Their side will rise.

Some objects have more mass than others. All objects and all forms of matter have mass. An object's mass does not change. If it changes shape, or moves to another place, its mass is still the same.

Rocks

Make a clay horse and record its mass. What if you change its shape to a clay bird? If you measure its mass again, it will be the same if you used all the clay.

Weight is different than mass. An object's weight can change depending on its location.

Feathers

200 milliliters

350 milliliters

Volume

Volume is the amount of space an object takes up. All forms of matter have volume. A measuring cup can be used to measure the volume of liquids and solids. The volume of liquids is measured in liters. Liters are metric units. Each liter contains one thousand milliliters.

Pour some water into a measuring cup. The cup's water level rises to 200 milliliters. That level is the water's volume. Then place an orange in the cup of water. The liquid rises to 350 milliliters. What has happened? The orange added 150 milliliters to the measure. That means that the volume of the orange below water is 150 milliliters.

Density and Buoyancy

All matter has density. **Density** is a measure of how much matter is in a space. Think about a bag of bricks and a bag of cotton balls. The bags are equal in volume. But the bricks have more mass. The bricks have a greater density than the cotton.

You can learn more about an object's density by observing buoyancy. **Buoyancy** is how well an object floats. It is a property of matter.

Drop a brick into a pool. Its high density makes it sink. The brick has little buoyancy. What if you drop a cork into a pool? Its low density makes it float. The cork has a lot of buoyancy.

Measuring Properties

Matter's different properties can be observed in many ways. For example, you can use a ruler to measure an object's length. A meter is the basic metric unit of length. There are 100 centimeters in a meter. A kilometer has 1,000 meters.

Rulers and tape measures can be used to find the length of common objects. How long is your arm? Is it longer or shorter than your friend's arm? By measuring the length of both arms, you can find out for sure whose arm is longer. Two other properties of matter that can be measured are mass and volume.

Matter can be a solid, liquid, or gas. By observing matter's properties, you can learn more about it.

Did you know that you can combine all three states of matter at once? Gather together a piece of paper, a straw, and paint. The paper and straw are solids. The paint is a liquid. And the air in your breath is a gas. Place a dab of paint on the paper. Then blow through the straw to move it around. You have just mixed three forms of matter! Everyday objects can be more interesting when you study their matter and properties.

Glossary

atom   the smallest particle of an element that still has the properties of that element

buoyancy   how well an object floats or sinks

density   a measure of the amount of matter in a certain amount of space

element   matter made of a single type of particle

mass   the amount of matter an object has

matter   anything that takes up space and has mass

periodic table   a table of all elements based on their properties

pressure   when something such as air pushes against another thing

property   a quality of matter that you can observe

volume   the amount of space an object takes up